You Are Designed to Be
SUCCESSFUL

FREDDIE FLOYD JR

ISBN 978-1-63630-132-7 (Paperback)
ISBN 978-1-63630-133-4 (Digital)

Covenant Books, Inc.
11661 Hwy 707
Murrells Inlet, SC 29576
www.covenantbooks.com

This book is dedicated to my beautiful wife, Katrina Floyd. I want to give you special thanks for being my support system in everything that I have done, you are truly the backbone of our relationship, and I love you so much.

To my daughter, Rayna Floyd, one whom I have seen grow from a little cute chubby girl to a beautiful young woman. May God continue to watch over you and direct your life.

My strength lies in you two, all that I do is to ensure your life is upgraded. "But if man provide not for his own, and especially for those of his own house, he hath denied the faith, and is worse than an infidel" (1 Timothy 5:8). Up to this point, I pray that I have lived up to that statement. Love you, ladies.

Contents ·

Preface

This book is about developing a relationship with the Creator, grow-ing your faith, and watching your life prosper because of your new understanding. The book brings us back to the Creator and shows us it's never too late to make a change and return back to God. I will show you how my life was changed simply because I returned back to the Father. My goal of this book is to put the focus back on God as we have turned our back on him and honestly we are trying to travel this journey alone. The word of God still works but we have some things we need to do to jumpstart what God has for us. My goal is to ensure you have understanding and there is no reason to think we're supposed to lack in any area of our life. With God all things are made possible if we believe and take action. God's word never returns without things happening.

For just as rain and snow fall from heaven and do not return without watering the earth, making it bud and sprout, and providing seed to sow and food to eat, so "My word that proceeds from God's mouth will not return to him empty, but it will accomplish what I please, and it will prosper where I send it" (Isaiah 55:11).

Acknowledgment · · · · · · · · · · · · · · · ·

How does a person say "thank you" when there are so many people to thank?

Obviously I have to thank my wonderful parents, Mr. Freddie and Mrs. Cathy Floyd

My older brother, Felix Floyd, who is the example I have modeled myself to be like growing up. He has a unique way of showing support but you always know you can count on him for anything and my love goes deep for that brother.

My aunt, Betty Stanley, what can I say about her? Being supportive is an understatement. It doesn't matter what we talk about from the Bible to just life, a negative word never comes out her mouth and that is a blessing in itself.

Joseph Maurice (Big Mo) from New Orleans. This guy was such an inspiration to me and to think all this time he thought I was just inspiring to him, all the while I was looking up to him as well. I want to challenge you, brother, never give up on you.

To *Cashema* Floyd, *Charita Floyd*, *Frederick Floyd*, I love you guys so much.

To my aunts and uncles, I say thank you for all your support.

Introduction ·

This book was created for all that have struggled and are still struggling with who they are. If you have ever wondered why things are
not going right in your life and find yourself comparing your life
to others, this is the book for you. Often times we just don't understand why we are where we are but we all have a purpose, we all
want answers to why we're not at our destiny. I can help with some
of those questions but are you willing to go on the journey that gets
you there? What you've been doing isn't working. Will you dare to
try something different?

Chapter 1

KNOWING GOD IS
HOW IT STARTS

> God is not a man, that he should lie, or a son
> of man that he should change his mind. Does
> he speak and not act? Does he promise and not
> fulfill?
>
> —Numbers 23:19

The very first thing we should learn is who is our creator and have
an understanding of the difference between him and man. Why is
this of importance? It's because we tend to trust in man and omit
what God says. This is why I started with that scripture. It destroys
all doubt that God and man are not the same. A man will fail you
over and over again. The Bible says, "Wisdom is the beginning: get
wisdom therefore: and above all thy possession gets an understanding." You cannot expect to have success with anything in life without
an understanding. You have to learn who you are, who your Father
in heaven is, and what your capabilities are. How can you expect to
have any of the blessings that God says you have access to if you don't
know him and aren't trying to know him? Do you not know we are
created for him, and really all we have to do is follow, and blessing
will come pouring in? The problem is we often want what comes
with the blessing and are not willing to put in the work to receive
the blessings. You see this example in almost every area of life in this
society. For an example, a person wants the results of losing weight

yet they would rather omit the work it takes in the gym or eating properly in order to get the quick results. Well you can't take any shortcuts with the Father because it's all about the condition of your heart and attitude. There are no shortcuts to success.

If we are honest with ourselves you would admit that at some point in your life you have wanted what someone else had, but when we found out what it took to get it our minds changed quickly due to our lack of willingness to go through that person's pain and misery. We just want right now. But yet we expect to have that abundant life we are promised in his word. Well I hate to disappoint you, but it takes effort on your part, especially if you weren't born into money. Within all of us, I believe there exists a strong desire to be known and to know others in some form or fashion. Today we see all types of advertising that promises ways to satisfy our cravings to know more, have more, and be more. However, the promises that come from the world will never satisfy you in the way that knowing God will. Following God is a simply strategy to success with your mind, body, and spirit. If we just open the Bible and start reading, it's a simple guide and it works just not overnight like the society may suggest. I know we are in the now era but it's a process; just like losing weight, it's a process. Have you ever wanted to lose twenty pounds? You go to the gym and a week later you still have that unwanted weight, you lost some but you're not where you want to be. It takes time, discipline, and effort. So, what is the key to truly knowing God? It's studying his word, and time. You see God moves in your life according to his speed, not ours.

First, it is imperative to understand that man, on his own, is incapable of truly knowing God because we have such a sinful nature. The Bible reveals to us that we are all sinful and that we fall short. Short of what, you may ask. It's short of his desires for us. He already knew we would struggle without him, which is why he left the door open for anyone who wishes to return to him and he would receive us. We are also told that the consequence of our sin is death and that we will perish eternally without God unless we accept and receive the promise of Jesus's sacrifice on the cross. So, in order to truly know God, we must first receive Him into our lives. "As many as received him, to them he gave the right to become children of God, even to those who believe in his name" (John 1:12). Nothing is of greater importance than understanding this truth when it comes to knowing God. Jesus makes it clear that he alone is the way to heaven and to a personal knowledge of God: "I am the way, and the truth, and the life; no one comes to the Father, but through him" (John 14:6).

We are created to love and to give, which can also lead to comfortable living, God says he shall supply all your needs according to his riches in glory, but notice by Christ Jesus his son. Now the first thing we have to understand and accept is that it says God will supply according to His riches and glory which means it all belongs to him and secondly by way of his son Jesus. This is what Jesus meant when he says I am the way, the truth, and the life.

You see, we as people tend to walk around thinking we're doing something, we take all the credit and just leave God out of the mix. How often have you had a conversation with a co-worker or a friend and they tell you about an accomplishment that they may have played a part in and it's "I did, I did, I did." And not only do they leave God out, they are not even giving credit to the people that helped them along the way. Talk about self-gratitude, right. God wants us to rely on him and not on our self. It's no wonder we struggle so much in this lifetime. God says acknowledge him and he will make your paths straight. All God wants from us is acknowledgement. You know when I was a kid I was taught to think we should never question God but because I had some things I wanted answered which just weren't making sense to me, such as if you're all powerful why are so many poor people out here? I mean they would seem like it was normal to be poor like that's just the way it is so I needed to know more about this God they were serving and why would he want us to be poor and homeless on purpose? It has to be something we did or didn't do. (Now another disclaimer, I am not speaking of people who have mental illness.) Healthy individuals, it just doesn't make sense right. (Notice I didn't say be wealthy.) This is a very important statement. Scripture says, "If you then, which are evil, can give to your earthly children good gifts, how much more shall your Father which is in heaven, give good things to them that ask him" (Matthew 7:11). God wants us to totally rely on him and to trust him, one of the issues that we as people tend to do is when we have a problem is go directly to man with our issues first and God second. That's a no-no. This is totally out the will of God. He says, "Come to me, all who are weary and heavy-laden, and I will give you rest" (Matthew 11:28). If you are not seeking God first, it's totally out of the elements of your success window. Remember it's all about understanding and since the world tends to dilute the word with its arrogance, you as an individual have a responsibility to yourself to study the word for yourself in order to understand what is true and what is not according to scripture. You will not know the full truth of God's word without studying it for yourself. He is giving you all the resources. You just have to take the next step—read his word.

As you begin to read God's word, allow me to bring something of importance to your attention that I think is often over looked. In the very first book of *Genesis,* it says God created! Not man. So we are created by God himself in his image, according to his likeness. God said, "Let us make man in our image according to our likeness, and let them rule" (Genesis 1:26). It's important before you move further that you understand God said let them, meaning both male and female. Consequently according to God's word he gave the same order to female to rule as he gave to man in the spirit form. "And God blessed them, and God said to them, Bring forth fruit, and multiply, and fill the earth, and subdue it, and rule over the fish of the sea, and over the fowl of the heaven, and over every beast that moved upon the earth" (Genesis 1:28). That passage alone is the first impression God gave us which shows success. God gave *you/us*. There was no gender bias you were designed to have with no efforts from ourselves. However due to the disobedience of the man, yes, let's call a spade a spade, it was man that actually failed because God instructed man not the woman. You don't really hear people quote that because again of the sinful nature of man. God told the fully formed man not to eat the forbidden fruit. So there it is—man was the hard-headed one. But, moving on, even with his failure, we are still designed to have success; only now it takes effort by way of choices in order to live the abundant life that God has promised. I will say this, when you know God and something horrible happens in your life, it's God that keeps you from taking your life, knowing God is what keeps you from leaping off a building. Knowing God in this context is having a relationship with him. Let's look at one example of Asaph. In *Psalm 73*, Asaph talks about how he was tempted to envy the wicked that seemed to have no cares and built their fortunes upon the backs of those they took advantage of. This is a prime example of walking by faith and not by sight because often when you see, we want to do. We see the riches that are being received by mistreating others, but then he considered their ultimate end. In contrast to what they sought after, he states what mattered to him: "Whom have I in heaven but you? And earth has nothing I desire besides you" (Psalm 73:25). To Asaph, a relationship with God mattered above all else in life. Without that relationship, life has no real purpose.

By design, God wants you to trust in him because he is our creator. He wants and needs us to depend on him for the things we need. It's better to trust in the Lord, than to have confidence in man. We all know that people are just what they are—people—and they feel they reserve the right to change their mind about things. While that part is true, God says he will not leave us or forsake us. God doesn't change his mind like man. God says heaven and earth will pass away, but his words will never pass away—the focus is on the word never. Doesn't that make you feel great? Even when you feel things are tough on you, you can take great pleasure in knowing God is still with you. God wants all of our attention and he will give you all of his.

We must talk with God and allow him the time to move on our behalf. We cannot be in such a hurry that we act on our own. When we pray, we ask God for answers. And if you don't hear anything, you do nothing. You must let God do the leading. Yes, I know we live in a fast-paced world where we want everything right now, you have heard of the saying that patience is a virtue and it really is. Patience reveals our faith in God's timing. If we cannot wait on God, we cannot expect to prosper throughout life.

We must sit down and study the Word to really have confidence in God and know we can hear him. Being that we are sprits, the Bible is food for our spirit. We have to feed the spirit daily just as you feed your natural body daily and as we spend time reading and meditating on scripture, we develop an even stronger spirit. Then we can hear God speaking to our heart—where he dwells in us—and make decisions based upon what he's leading us to do, not just what we may think, feel, or want.

When you go beyond what you want, what you think, and what you feel, and do what the Word and the Spirit of God tell you to do, you are able to develop good habits and break bad ones. You come to a place where the blessings of God—his righteousness, peace, and joy—are overflowing in your life.

Life can be simple and peaceful when we come to God like little children and say, "God, I don't want to live like this any longer on my own. I want to trust you. When I don't know what to do, I'll trust you. When I don't understand why, I'll trust you. I'll do my part with your help, and when I'm done, I'll trust you to do the rest."

> Trust in the *Lord* with all your heart and lean not on your own understanding; in all your ways acknowledge him, and he will make your paths straight. Do not be wise in your own eyes. (Proverbs 3:5–7)

That verse right there was a mouthful in itself. Don't be a know it all. Trusting God means making yourself vulnerable.

To be perfectly clear with you, trusting in God has nothing to do with whether or not bad things happen to you or you want go through any trials; in fact, it's just the opposite. Scripture says that, "For he make his sun rise on the evil and on the good, and sends rain on the just and on the unjust" (Matthew 5:45), so you will go through things but it's how you deal with those things which sets you apart from the rest of the world. God's got you in the palm of his hand if we rely on him. In fact, Romans speaks about tribulation and how we should glorify in it, not because of what we're going through but because it works patience in your life, and with patience comes experience, and with experience, hope, knowing God will step in if we continue to trust in him.

One of the best examples I have found in scripture of somebody who trusted God is Job. Job is such an excellent example. Job was a very wealthy man who had it all, a family, livestock, and even servants, and he lost it all, I mean everything. In fact, Job was such a just man that the Bible called him perfect and there were none like him at that time. When this happened to Job, he was angry, quite naturally, and I am sure he wondered what he had done so bad to lose everything and he yelled out, "Why did I not perish at birth, and die as I came from the womb" (Job 3:11). You see this was a great example. Job got mad yet he didn't stray from God and turn his back on him or lose his faith as most do today because of a lack of understanding in how God goes about his business in our lives.

Despite everything that happened to Job, through all the pain and suffering, he never stopped worshipping God. He did speak these words, "Naked came I out of my mother's womb and naked shall I return thither" (Job 1:21). Job came to the realization that knowing God is better than having answers to all of our questions. You see nowhere in scripture does it say when things happen to you that you are supposed to know why. God is in control always and with Job, in the end, after he showed God that he would not turn his back on him, *God then restored Job and made him twice as prosperous as he was before.* All praises to the most high. When Job faced his own problems in life, his response was to ultimately fear God and shun evil. We have to submit our heart in full obedience to God. Not rely on human wisdom and understanding. In every area of our life, acknowledge God and act according to his wisdom, and he will make the right path—his path—clear to you. Don't be wise according to your own wisdom. Instead, reverence God and his ways and avoid sin the best you can because this world that we live in is sinful and it's always going to have traps that try to lure you away from God. But if you hold on to the never-changing God himself, he will restore us.

We must learn to submit our heart in full obedience to God. Don't prop yourself up with human wisdom and understanding. In every area of your life, acknowledge God. To acknowledge is an act of recognizing God's full lordship in our lives and then we must act according to his wisdom, and he will make the right path—his path—clear to you. Don't be wise according to your own wisdom. Instead, reverence God and his ways. God is always on your side and he is waiting for your return. We just have to reach out for him.

Chapter 2 ·

FAITH

> And Jesus answered saying unto them, "Have
> faith in God."
> —Mark 11:22

I wanted to start this chapter off by showing you that even Jesus says to have faith in God. Now that we know who God is, we now need to know what it takes to please him because pleasing God is what opens doors to his given. We can find this in *Hebrews 11:6*, which says it is impossible to please God without faith. So how do we find out what faith is? We should always first go to the Bible to see what faith entails. "Faith is the substance of things hoped for, the evidence of things not seen" (Hebrews 11:1). This verse tells us that faith is an evidence that we have regarding something that allows us to be able to act on it as if it were assured of happening. But where does assurance come from? A lot of people have the above scripture memorized but then when you ask the question about where does faith come from, you either get an "I don't really know" or it comes from within with the implication that faith is something we develop ourselves.

So let us go to the Bible and see if it tells us where faith comes from. It amazes me how so much in this world is derived from the Bible. *Romans 12:3* says God has allotted to each a measure of faith. It is God that gives all of us a certain amount of faith but guess what, just like a plant that needs water to grow so does your faith; it must be watered so it may grow. So how do you water your faith you may ask, well it's simple. You must hear the word and receive the word, which is your water just like the plant. This is very important to understand as you begin your journey of success. "Jesus, the author and perfecta of faith" (*Hebrews 12:2*). So, it's God according to his word that gives a measure of faith and it's Jesus who perfects that very faith. Those two scriptures clearly tell us that faith is not something that we do or a presence of mind that we develop, but that faith is a gift from God.

"Faith comes from hearing and hearing by the word of Christ" (*Romans 10:17*). So, faith is a gift from God that we receive from the word of *God*, which in this dispensation we get from the Bible rather than from a burning bush. So, in his time, he will allot faith to us as needed from his word, the Bible. Scripture also tells us that faith can grow as in *2 Corinthians 10:15*, so as we study the word, God can add to our faith. Studying his word is something we all must do, and your faith will begin to grow as needed. It doesn't matter if you read something small daily, you need to feed your spirit.

For most, we are taught that we should go to church and I do believe in attending church services. Actually, I love church as it is where I find my peace of mind but we have to read for ourselves and as we study the word, God can add to our faith. This is simply amazing to me. All we have to do is read and study and our faith will grow as you mature. So, faith comes from hearing, and hearing the word of God, but faith without some sort of acting is dead according to scripture. Faith is indeed a gift from God; however, actions or our work is just to ignite our faith by listening and studying his word— they go hand in hand.

We clearly see from the above verses that faith is not of our doing for that would be a works-based salvation and we know that salvation is surely not from works. "For by grace you have been saved through faith—and that's not of ourselves, faith is the free gift of God" (Ephesians 2:8). Scripture also says, *"A man is justified by faith."* We read in *Romans 9:32* that Israel did not arrive at righteousness because they did not pursue righteous by faith but as though it were by works. If we must get our own faith, then justification is by works and again we know that is not correct. I have also pointed out that *"Jesus is the author and perfecter of faith,"* which fits in nicely with

what we have already seen. Jesus is not only the author—the origina-
tor of faith—he is also the one who perfects it in us.

So, up to this point, we have learned (1) that we must know
God, who is our Creator and he gave us without any sweat or efforts
the command to rule male and female according to his word; however to know God is not enough to get all his blessing that we are
to receive on an individual basis, (2) we also must have faith as his
word says its impossible to please God without it. When our physical
bodies were formed, everything we needed was given to us—again
that's male and female. As we grow in our own journey, I think it's
important to understand that in the beginning God spoke to both
male and female spirits, because, ladies, you are in that same setting
to be successful as well and you cannot allow anyone to steal from
you what God has designated for you to have. *1 Corinthians 3:14* says
every man shall receive his own reward according to his own labor.
In this context, God is not a respect of person. In other words, he
wasn't just speaking to men. So, ladies, you have your own journey
to success. I just wanted to make that point clear.

Some may say, "I know God and I have faith, so why am I
still broke and barely making it?" The answer to this very important
question started with Adam and Eve disobeying God and being cast
out of the garden of Eden, which subsequently is when sin entered
into the world. There was no sin in this world until man decided
to disobey God. Some would ask what is considered sin. According
to scripture, all sin can be traced back to this, "For all that is in the
world, (as *the lust of the flesh, the lust of the eyes, and the pride of life*) is
not of the Father but is of the world" (*1 John 2:16*). Hmm you may
say. Three little issues of life make up sin, can you believe that all
things of the Bible that is sin come in the form of those three state-
ments? Lust of the flesh, lust of the eyes, and the pride of life. Wow,
right. If you don't believe that, let's take a closer look at them and
break them down individually:

Lust of the flesh:

Lust is any sinful desire that is not contrary to the will of God.
Premarital sex is a big one. In fact, God says his will is that we abstain
from fornication (unmarried sex) (*1 Corinthians 7:9*) for it's better to

marry than to burn. Paul says being unmarried and having the ability to abstain from fornication is a gift because not everyone can go without sex because we are covered with flesh and in the flesh is sin, so if we focus on our flesh there is a price to pay. The Bible says the works of the flesh are adultery, fornication, uncleanness, lasciviousness, idolatry, witchcraft, hatred, and a list of others including being drunk *(Galatians 5:19)*. These things will destroy you over time.

Lust of the eyes:

This simply means we desire what we see. In scripture, the eyes are the primary organ of perception and often the principal avenue of temptation. *Proverbs 27:20* says the eyes of man are never satisfied. So, we must constantly work on ourselves to do better, to be better, and God is our avenue. This was also part of the commandment do not covet. The lust of the eye is very problematic for most all as we tend to gravitate to what our eyes show us. It's as if you're a key and you see this shiny stone from afar and you're drawn to it. Thank God that he is a forgiver as we all will spend a life time asking forgiveness for this one.

The boastful pride of life:

Describes the arrogant spirit of self-sufficiency. It expresses the desire for recognition, applause, status, and advantage in life. The phrase describes the pride in what life can offer you.

This goes back to why God wants us to rely on him one hundred percent because he knows these are things we cannot conquer on our own. Which is why he is saying in *Romans 3:23*, for all have sinned and fall short of God's glory. We cannot begin to think we can do this on our own. What we must learn to do is admit this and rely on God's forgiveness, we do have the ability to make choices whether we want to believe this or not. We just have to trust God and believe he will make a way out of no way. We all fall short and there hath no temptation taken you, but such as is common to man which means you're not the first to go through pain, someone else conquered it, and so can you. God is faithful, who will not suffer you to be tempted above that ye are able; but will with the temptation also make a way to escape, that ye may be able to bear it (1 Corinthians 10:13). Stop being so hard on yourself, God has you.

Chapter 3 · · · · · · · · · · · · · · · · · · ·

WE MUST REPENT

> And they went out, and preached that men
> should repent.
>
> —Mark 6:12

We live in a world where there are rules we must abide by, it's no different in the Bible except that God is willing to provide you with so much more and money isn't the providing that I am speaking about. Yes, money is a part of our success but from your Father's standpoint. God's rules are only in place to protect you and increase your life. As scripture says, it is the Lord our God who gives us the power to obtain wealth. However, we have to take some sort of action of our own.

Let's talk about the differences in repentance shall we:

According to King James study Bible, there are two Greek words used to characterize repentance in the New Testament that I will bring your attention to. (1.) The verb metamelomai is used as a change of mind, such as to produce regret or even remorse because you have sinned, but not necessarily a change of heart. This word is used with reference to the repentance of Judas. "Then Judas, which had betrayed him, when he saw that he was condemned, repented himself, and brought again the thirty pieces of silver to the chief priests and elders" (Matt. 27:3), (2.) Metanoeo, meaning to change one's mind and purpose, as the "result of after knowledge."

If you refer to the book of Ezekiel, it speaks that if a wicked person turns away from all his sins that he has committed, God is telling us to basically stop doing those things that you know bothers me and return to me, start over and God will then return to you. If your humbled heart repents of your wrongdoing, God will return to you and he will simply restore you. It's really that simple for God because he is a forgiving God, but the test is for us. Do we want what God has to offer us? That's the real question.

Repent simply means to turn away from doing the sins, we have stop and start over. The Bible teaches that repentance is essential to salvation. One cannot truly believe unless he repents, and one cannot truly repent unless he believes. These two go hand in hand with worshiping. *Acts 11:18* and *2 Peter 3:9* are two of the many verses that teach that repentance is necessary for salvation. There is no doubt that all men from Adam on up have to repent in order to have a right relationship with God. The importance of repentance is demonstrated by the fact that men of every biblical age preached it. Now let me add that just because you repented doesn't mean you want have to deal with the consequences. As some older people would say, if you dig your hole, you know you have to lie in. That is just a figure of speech meaning you have to deal with the punishment. Here are just a few examples of great men either repenting or teaching repentance.

Jesus Christ himself emphasized its importance when he said, "Except ye repent, ye shall all like-wise perish" (Luke 13:3).

John the Baptist preached it when he said, "Repent ye, and believe the gospel" (Mark 1:15).

Paul preached it, "Testifying both to the Jews, and also to the Greeks, repentance toward God, and faith toward our Lord Jesus Christ" (Acts 20:21).

John spoke of its necessity, "Repent and do the first works; or else I will come unto thee quickly, and will remove thy candlestick out of his place, except thou repent" (Revelation 2:5).

We read in Acts, "but now commandant all men everywhere to repent" (Acts 17:30).

As you see repentance is a real big deal when you're getting a right relationship with God, as it says it's a commandment. Essentially, repentance is simply that process by which a person who is away from God recognizes that situation and goes back to God.

Repentance is something that God demands of you. It is basically a U-turn. Instead of going away from God or ignoring him, you turn around, go to him, and choose to give him his rightful place in your life. Repentance, therefore, has more to do with your will than with your feelings. You may feel deep sorrow about certain things that you regret, or you may not, but the real issue is whether you go back to where you belong. "If my people, which are called by my name, shall humble themselves, and pray, and seek my face, and turn from their wicked ways; then will I hear from heaven, and will forgive their sin, and will heal their land" (2 Chronicles 7:14). One thing I would like to add is this, although repentance is highly important in your walk with Christ, I beg you to please don't forget to be baptized. Baptism is a symbolic death and resurrection in Christ Jesus.

All throughout scripture it teaches that repentance and baptism go hand in hand in order to receive the Holy Ghost. According to Matthew 28:19, it appears to be a commandment from Jesus himself. Jesus came and spoke to them saying, "All power is given unto me in heaven and in earth. Go ye therefore, and teach all nations, (everyone) baptizing them in the name of the Father, and of the Son, and of the Holy Ghost: Teaching them to observe all things whatsoever I have commanded you: and, lo, I am with you always, *even* unto the end of the world." Peter, following Jesus instructions, said unto them, "Repent, and be baptized every one of you in the name of Jesus Christ for the remission of sins, and ye shall receive the gift of the Holy Ghost."

So, the demand of Jesus to repent goes to all the nations. Why? Because we are all sinners. *1 John* says it best. "If we say that we have no sin, we deceive ourselves, and the truth is not in us" (1 John 1:8). It comes to us, whoever we are and wherever we are, and lays claim on us. This is the demand of Jesus to every single soul: Repent and be baptized in the name of the Father, the Son, and the Holy Ghost. God is teaching us what it takes to be closer to him. If we would just "Draw nigh to him, he will draw nigh to us" (James 4:8).

It's simply a matter of choices. He gives us guidance and he will leave it up to us to follow. He will not pressure you. However, when you find yourself struggling and can't see a way out, try God on for size. He promises to never leave you and if you decide to return to him, he will then return to you and heal your lands. He is not just talking about the lands he is speaking about all areas of your life. He says if. Which indicate choice? We will speak more about choices in the next the chapter.

Chapter 4 ·

FREEDOM OF CHOICES

Often the word choice is used in a negative connotation that you don't give it much real value. A case in point when it is used negatively is when a person says, "Look what you made me do." Yes, blaming others are high on the to-do list when dealing with someone other than yourself, but have you ever asked yourself, "Could I have decided not to do that?" Probably not because blaming others comes easier than taking responsibility for our own actions. The blame started with Adam and Eve. We have all heard the story of God telling Adam not to eat the forbidden fruit. Well as you could imagine, Adam blamed Eve, and even blamed the serpent.

Most of us, not all, have a hard time taking responsibility for what we did or didn't do. When dealing with God, he makes it so easy but it's our own sinful nature that would rather lie about it. A person really thinks God is going to force his will on you, but he doesn't, he always gives you choices. I once heard an acquaintance tell me that if God wanted me to do something, he would make me do it. I must beg to differ on that one. You see, looking back to the garden of Eden, in a time where God furnished so to speak as the home of the first man created, you will see the beginning of 'freedom of choice' where Adam and Eve chose to eat what was then the forbidden fruit of the garden. It was their choice! As my acquaintance said, "God would make him." Well, he didn't make them. In fact, he told them, "You may have freely all you lay your eyes on, except the forbidden fruit." So clearly that was a choice. There is only one instance in the life of man where God made the choice for you, God created Adam, a man. No choice, God created Eve, a woman. Neither of them had any choice either to be born or as to their sex. We don't choose our family So in that example the choices were decided for them. Outside of those very few instances, choices are to be made all around us. People say I have no choice but that is the one thing that has the most power over our lives and it's the freedom to choose. The sooner we stop blaming others for our choice, the sooner we can walk into our destiny.

Jesus says, *"I am come that they might have life, and have it in abundance"* (*John 10:10*), which means having plenty of. So if this is Jesus's word, again the question is why are we lacking anything? It's simple, it comes down to choices. I truly believe with all my heart that we are today where we are based on the choices we made or didn't make. You see choices determine your future. God says he will supply all your needs according to his riches in glory. Now let's analyze that statement for a moment. We have to continue to look back at the beginning to know what God said which will give us the strength go where we're supposed to go in life. Let's go back to what we have learned.

Step 1) We need to know God. He is our creator. This means he created not just us but the entire universe. He has it all, for by him were all things were created. That's scripture, that's his word, should you not believe that please refer to this verse, *"The earth is the Lord's, and all it contains, the world, and those who dwell in it"* (*Psalms 24:1*). *That's Old Testament* and for those thinking that the Old Testament meant nothing you find this again further in the New Testament in *1 Corinthians 10:26* and *Hebrews 2:10* saying the same things so the Old is transferred to the New, please understand that.

Step 2) It's so important to have faith. He himself (God) says it's impossible to please him without it and we know it comes from God where he says, *"God hath dealt to everyman the measure of faith"* (*Romans 12:3*). We learned faith can grow if you read and study his word where it says faith comes by hearing and hearing of the word of God.

Step 3) As required, we must all repent, ask for forgiveness, and turn over a new leaf of doing things. We cannot put on clean clothes and have the same dirt on use and expect to feel clean, I'm just saying.

One thing I want to add before going further is you have to believe in yourself. However, it's my belief that once you learn who God says you are, you will understand your true strength but I didn't want to leave that part out.

Let's look deeper as to how choices help to mold our future or hinder or slow down the abundant living we so desire. Choices are huge in life but we often take a choice very lightly. At times, they don't seem very significant. But those choices set in motion a series of events which shape our lives. Sometimes people make unwise choices, which aren't vital in themselves, but they can oftentimes lead to tragedies. Let me provide an example of an unwise choice. I want to think of something that's so common in today's sinful world. Let's talk about married men that cheat. Let's be clear that I do not condone cheating; however, it's still alive well in society. So he decides to take a woman's number, you don't think much about it at the time but when the wife finds out about it would have a lot of explaining to do (unwise choice). Or how about when you decide to ride with a friend whom you know has been drinking, which results in a serious accident or maybe even loss of life? Those choices show the possibility of something bad happening a mile away and yet both examples could have been avoided. The Bible couldn't have put it more precise when it says, "I call heaven and earth to witness against you today, that I have set before you, life and death, the blessing and the curse" (*Deuteronomy 30:15*). He is saying choose wisely in order that you may live, not only you but also your children after you. So, you see, God is always giving us the choice but we're not always listening, which is why the curses came in the first place.

In the story of Abram, later named Abraham, and Lot, we have yet another good example of how a choice can lift you up or tear you down. Abram was a wealthy man; Lot was well off too. Their *increased wealth* leads to *increased strife* because there simply wasn't enough land for each of them where Abram had been previously occupying; not to mention the Canaanites and the Perizzites were there as well. They didn't have that problem before. Who on earth says that money fixes all problems? Some of the most unhappy families I know didn't seem to be unhappy until they came into money. So, as I said, the increased strife led to *increased responsibility* for choices. Lot wasn't just deciding for himself. His family, his servants, and their families would be affected by his decision. The increased responsibility for choices led to either *increased wickedness* (in Lot's case, choosing Sodom) or *increased blessing* (in Abram's case, choosing Canaan). I want to bring your attention to Genesis verse 8, when Abram said to Lot, "Please let there be no strife between you and me because we are brothers." Coming just after the statement about the Canaanites and Perizzites being in the land, this may point to Abram's concern about how their strife would affect the witness to the pagans around them. How can God's people bear witness for Him if the world sees them fighting among themselves?

Abram had a right to choose whatever land he wanted and let Lot take the leftovers. He was the older, the chief of the clan. God had promised the land to Abram, not to Lot. (Note, by the way, that even though Abram and Lot both had the freedom to choose, God's sovereign purpose to give the land to Abram overruled their choices.) But Abram graciously yielded his rights and trusted God to give him his portion. What mattered to Abram was, "We are brothers." He valued his relationship with Lot over his right to choose the best land.

So much strife could be avoided in the family and in the church if we would put a premium on our relationships, set aside our rights, and let the Lord take care of us. The next time you are about to quarrel with someone (and quarrelling is a choice we make), stop and think about whether the quarrel is rooted in godly principles or in selfishness. Sometimes we need to confront sin or take a stand for the truth, even though it causes conflict. But be careful! It's easy to justify selfishness by calling it righteous anger. The general rule is, "Let us pursue the things which make for peace and the building up of one another" (*Romans 14:19*).

Now as you very well know Abram was what I call a Gods' man, meaning he was down with God by faith. Abram had already renounced everything visible and opted for the unseen promises of God. So he had no need, as Lot did, to choose by sight. There is a deliberate contrast between verses 10 and 14. In verse 10, Lot *lifted up his eyes* and chose the land which looked the best to him. He took off for the good life and left Abram literally in the dust, in dusty Canaan, where there had just been a severe famine. In verse 14, as Abram is standing there wondering if he did the right thing (and perhaps Sarah was asking him the same question), God tells him to *lift up his eyes* and look in every direction. All the land he can see will be his. Perhaps as Abram was looking around, his eyes fell down to the dusty soil on which he was standing. So the Lord says, "Do you see all that dust? I'll make your descendants as the dust of the earth, so that if anyone can number the dust of the earth, then your descendants can also be numbered."

Lot chose by sight and ended up in the pits so to speak. He escaped Sodom with the clothes on his back and fades out living in a cave. The things he saw and got didn't bring him the lasting happiness he expected. Abram chose by faith, not by sight, and ended up spiritually and financially blessed, seeing and possessing by faith the whole land of Canaan, although he died owning only a burial plot. Lot lived for greed and came up empty. Abram lived for God and came up full.

As believers, we are to live by faith in the promises of God. When we face decisions, we take God into account and make those decisions in line with his promises and principles, not the immediate gratification of the flesh. We deny ungodliness and worldly desires in light of the blessed hope of Christ's return (*Titus 2:11–13*), trusting that his promises concerning eternity are true.

The Lord Jesus said, "Seek *first* the kingdom of God and his righteousness and all these things will be added to you" (Matt. 6:33). Most of us want to seek the other things first and add the kingdom of God later in our spare time. The next time you face a decision that involves a major commitment of your time or a move to a different location, make the decision based on how it will affect you and your family's commitment to the kingdom, not on financial factors alone. If the extra hours and the move will bring you more money, you need to ask, "Why do we want more money? Is it so we can give more to missions?" If the bottom line is that you want more money because you want more things, then you're not seeking God's kingdom.

So make your choices based on God's principles: relationships over rights, godliness over greed, fellowship with God over the world's approval, and faith in God's promises over immediate pleasure from the world. Because if you have God and his promises, you have everything. So, seek him first, and all else is yours.

Did you know that Genesis 13 is the first mention of wealth in the Bible? Wealth can be a blessing, but we need to recognize something that isn't said very often in our prosperous culture: *Wealth is a dangerous blessing! I think I even read that in a book by Robert Kiyosaki, he spoke about the problem of no money as well as having too much money and they both can be an issue.* Increased wealth always results in increased potential either for evil or for good. As the word says to whom much is given, much shall be required (*Luke 12:48*). When your income increases, so does your accountability to God.

We need to pay serious attention to the biblical warnings about wealth. As Jesus watched the rich young ruler walk away, he observed, "How hard it is for those who are wealthy to enter the kingdom of God!" (*Luke 18:24*). The apostle Paul said, "Those who want to get rich fall into temptation and a snare and many foolish and harmful desires which plunge men into ruin and destruction.

"For the love of money is the root of all evil" (1 Tim. 6:9–10).

Although money is needed you really have to be careful with your desire to obtain it, you shouldn't want to do anything for money just to have it, this is where we often go wrong in our quest to get money. One thing you don't hear people quote often is that money answers all things. With that being said, here is an example of money answering all things. If you go out on a date and your date is acting up, if you have money, you can get you an Uber to get home. If you're hungry, you can buy something to eat. So yes, it's needed but don't sell your soul for it. One of the more important choices you can make is stewardship and I will discuss this in the next chapter. Money used properly can be a very fulfilling thing in your life but if not, it can be very hurtful to others as well. God never designed his people to not help the less fortunate; nowhere in scripture will you find that.

Chapter 5

STEWARDS OF OUR MONEY

Money is a hot topic upon the mouths of everyone. Some will only talk about money and others will pretend we are not supposed to have it, like it's a bad thing or something. But let's be clear, it's needed to survive in the world we are living. In fact it's so important that the Bible even says, "Money answers all things" (*Ecclesiastes 10:19*). Now that's the thing, it doesn't mean your problems will go away. It simply means it's needed to make purchases on things you need in this lifetime. People hold money in such a high regard that the Bible references money and possessions more than Jesus talked about love. Let that sink in for a moment.

That's pretty amazing and we all know how important love is to God. Scripture says God is love. However we simply misuse the money God allows us to have which is why it's spoken of so often. A major problem that we have in today's society is how we handle the things that God provides for us. We always want more but we are not being good stewards of what we have. God indeed is a provider. Simply put, "My God will supply all your needs according to his riches in glory in Christ Jesus" (*Philippians 4:19*). That word in Christ Jesus is the key, while prosperity seekers are always looking for money or possessions to miraculously arrive, we should take a closer look at what God desires to provide for us. You must ask yourself, what are your needs? Food, clothing, shelter, transportation. God differentiates between our needs and our wants because he knows that where our treasure is, there our heart is also.

He wants us to know that this world is not our home and that part of what we need is to shift our focus to the eternal life while still living this one. God is concerned with every part of our being: spirit, soul, and body. So the ways God provides for us are beyond anything we can ask or imagine. Let's take this a step further. *"From everyone who has been given much, much will be demanded or required" (Luke 12:47–48).* So if God is to give you something or, to use a better term, to allow you to have something you must take care of it, especially a job. It amazes me as to how many males don't want to work, can you believe it? God has said, not only in the Old Testament but again in the New Testament, that a man that doesn't work shouldn't eat. Here is a small parable for you to apply to your own life. How can you expect to get money out of an ATM if you haven't put anything in it first? You want money to come out it, but life doesn't work like that. That's all God is telling us. If we put our trust in God, he is willing to provide more than you can ever imagine.

Let's look at one great example of not wasting what God gives you. Mathew 14:20 reads that they all ate as much as they wanted, and afterward, the disciples picked up twelve baskets of leftovers. When God provides, he always gives you more than enough and that is how you are able to be blessing to others.

Today we live in a society that every time you turn on the television someone is attempting to sell you something and this makes it all the more important to understand that wanting something is different from needing something and those that pretend they don't know the difference tend to have financial problems. In fact, most people that struggle with their finances buy what they want and struggle to get their needs.

Your faith will work if you work it. Meaning you can't ask God for a job and not apply, you can't expect to get a promotion without going to work. As I said, faith will work if you work it. God is your provider and he wants you to have, but you have to take care of what he allows you to have in order to get increase. We all have to learn how to be good stewards and it doesn't come over night. Here is a great example of being a good steward of what God allowed you to have. In *Matthew 25:20–21*, it shows a great analogy as to what stewardship is all about concerning money. And he who had received the five talents came forward, bringing five talents more, saying, "Master, you delivered to me five talents; here I have made five talents more. Do you see the increase?" His master said to him, "Well done, good and faithful servant. You have been faithful over a little; I will set you over much. Enter into the joy of your master." You have to control the money you earn and not allow the money to control you. Keep your life free from the love of money, and be content with what you have, for he has said, "I will never leave you or forsake you."

I am telling you, right now we need to return to God and refocus because God is a provider and he says, "Ask and you shall receive." God is saying, "I am here for you," kind of like what the world calls a tit-for-tat concept. God is saying if you do I will do, but to the third power. Listen to what it says in Proverbs, "There is treasure to be desired and oil in the dwelling of the wise; but a foolish man spends it up" (Proverbs 21:20). There is an abundance of all things but you cannot be foolish with it.

Chapter 6 ·

WE ARE HERE TO GIVE

This is what being a child of God is all about. We are supposed to be givers by nature. Every Sunday at church when we are about to give, my pastor then would have a saying that goes like this, "These are my given hands, and my given hands are a micro-reflection of my receiving hands, and because I am a giver I decree and declare this is not a season but a lifestyle of increase, options, and overflow." That simple motivation meant so much to me way back then, and still does. We do this so we can get in our heads as people of God we are supposed to give and he says you should never go into a worship service without giving something.

I believed him; however, I have never been one of those that you just tell me something and I do it. I was always that person that asked why. I mean it sounded good but why? I turn to scripture to get my answers because it is and has always been God's plan for us to follow his word. Especially now we are living in a world where people are turning their back once again from God and relying more on what man says. To be clear scripture says, "But the word of the Lord endured forever" (*1 Peter 1:25*). The last word is my focus. *Forever.* Now that is in the New Testament. I bring that to light because unless there was a new covenant I have missed, this was the last covenant and it still stands today.

I often heard people say they are not giving to the church because they don't know what the pastor is doing with their money, which is understandable. However, if you focus more on the word of God that is being sent forth and not on your own reasoning, you wouldn't have a problem giving. In both the Old and New Testament, "Be ye holy as I am holy" (*Leviticus 11:44/1 Peter 1:16*), means he will be our God and we will be his people. It means to be set apart from the rest of the world.

God himself is a natural giver. That is the first thing he did when he created us in Genesis, it says he gave us. So we know God is a giver. Scripture also says he will supply all of our needs. That is just another wonderful example of his giving. We just want more as a people. And you can have more because he wants us to have. That's a core value of me writing this book to help you understand that if you're broke and barely making it, it's not God's intention for his people to go without. I can show you this in scripture. Contrary to the popular teaching that we all are to be rich, I am simply teaching that with proper choices you can have a comfortable life, including your finances.

Jesus said it best in John, where it says, "The thief comes only to steal and kill and destroy; I came that they may have life, and have it abundantly" (*John 10:10*). This very statement again leads me to believe truly that following God's word, you should at the very least have your needs taken care of, period. Before I offend someone I must reiterate God's word in my earlier chapter that the rain does pour on the just and the unjust so you may follow God's word to a T and still lose everything as Job did however. If you continue to worship God, he will restore you. That's just a fact.

"Whoever is generous to the poor lends to the Lord, and he will repay him for his deed" (Proverbs 19:17).

This is like the verse where Jesus said if you help someone else, you are helping him because if someone is generous to the poor, they are in a sense, lending to the Lord. The Lord promises to "repay [them] for [their] deed" so this is a win-win situation. Help someone in need and the Lord himself will repay you and remember, focus more on others instead of your own self. When God blesses you, you are supposed to turn around and bless someone else that is why you continue to have. If you know anything about the rich, you will notice they are constantly giving to charities or something. Now for a poor-minded person, the first thing you think of is the reason the rich give is so they can use it as a tax write-off. But who are you to say so? The focus should be on you, yourself, and you should ask yourself what you are giving. The focus should always be on the giving part, from the heart, and judging someone is not going to get you where you want to go—it's the giving. God says, "Prove me," in other words, he says try me and see if I want to open up heaven's doors for you and get this, he says, "Pour out not many, not plenty," He says blessings, plural, that you will not have enough room to receive it. Now tell me that's not in the abundant form. In this context, God was referring to tithing and offering robbing God of what rightly belongs to him. In almost all instances, when God refers to giving, he is speaking of giving to the less fortunate. It's a big deal in God's eyes to help others. It's a lifetime endeavor as the Bible says. The less fortunate (poor) will always be among us always so we can have plenty of practice giving.

When I tell you God don't play about the poor or less fortunate try this one for size. Leviticus 19:10 makes it clear that we are here not only to give God praise but to help the poor. God told the Israelites back then they were living in a more agricultural time when they would harvest the fields, "Do not clean your fields but you are to leave a certain amount for the poor and strangers. I am the *Lord* your God." If that verse doesn't help you understand better that we should have a giving spirit, what will it take?

The Bible is clearly showing us how to receive a more abundant life. Let's look at a few more verses to instruct us to give and this truly should become a way of life. I remember when I was a kid and I had me a piece of peppermint in my pocket about to eat, there was a young pastor that asked if he could have my peppermint. Of course the selfish mentality I had then says, "No way, I only have one." And he reached inside his car and pulled out a bag of peppermint and he kindly said, "I didn't want it. I was just trying to see where your heart was." Even back then, God was teaching me a lesson on the art of giving. He speaks to us in all sorts of ways.

Below you find but a few scriptures that teaches about giving:
Luke 6:38

Give, and you will receive. Your gift will return to you in full—pressed down, shaken together to make room for more, running over, and poured into your lap. The amount you *give* will determine the amount you get back. You are not to have a selfish mindset and expect riches or great success.

2 Corinthians 9:7

Each one must give as he has decided in his heart, not reluctantly or under compulsion, for God loves a cheerful giver.

Acts 20:35

In all things I have shown you that by working hard in this way we must help the weak and remember the words of the Lord Jesus, how he himself said, "It is more blessed to give than to receive."

Proverbs 11:24

Give freely and become wealthier; be stingy and lose everything.

My baby brother Frederick Leon has always shown a sign of this verse. He will give his all to anyone and have nothing left but in some way, somehow God always came through for him as he was never in need of anything. But understand, God never said wealth is always money. Having all the things that you need makes you a blessed person beyond measure and we need to be able to recognize blessings outside of finances. We focus on money such that we don't pay attention to our needs being met. Remember God says, "I will supply all of your needs." Again God's words never return to him void. We just have to understand that he is meeting your needs. When we read and study the Bible, we have to read it slowly and never skip over words or you will miss out on so much that God intends for us to get in order to get his blessing.

Looking at the Interests of Others

Let each of you look not only to his own interests,
but also to the interests of others. (Philippians 2:4)

The interests of others ought to be our interests too. Certainly we look out for ourselves but how can we turn a blind eye when others have needs. There is a certain genius in generosity because God gives back what we let pass through our hands. But if we hold tight with clinched fists what we have, God cannot pour more into hands that are already clinging tightly to what they hold.

Sharing Pleases God

> Do not neglect to do good and to share what you have, for such sacrifices are pleasing to God. (Hebrews 13:16)

The converse of this is true: if we fail to do good and do not share what we have, we are neglecting others. Sharing what you have are the types of personal sacrifices that are pleasing to God. When the Scriptures talk about pleasing God, then we know it must be important. This was part of the reason that the early church grew so rapidly; "All the believers were together and had everything in common. They sold property and possessions to give to anyone who had need" (*Acts 2:44–45*). What we have been blessed with by God should be a blessing too for others.

We have to acknowledge him and in all our ways, he will direct our paths. If you want to do better, be better, live better. Return to God. I mean he is our creator and he should know a little something about us and what is good for us. He is waiting on us. For those who want wealth, again it's God that gives us the ability to obtain it. If we would just seek ye first the kingdom of God and his righteousness, then all of those things we desire will be added unto us. Scripture says if we delight ourselves in him, he will give us the desires of our heart. You see there is no getting away from giving God the glory if you want to be successful. It's your God-given right to have full access to what God has for you. Now that's for you and only you. You cannot have what another has, unless you are willing to go through what that person or persons have gone through. We ought to not look upon another and focus on you.

Conclusion ·

God designed his people to follow him and obey his principles. In doing so, he ensures we are well taken care of. He is able to do exceedingly, abundantly above all that we can ask or think. But we have to get our attitude toward money straight, and it will help straighten out almost every other area in our life. Each of us has something to give. The Bible says every man shall receive his own reward according to his own labor. No one can get your portion for you. And that's the bottom line. I hope this book blesses you as well as it has blessed me in writing it. All praise to the most high.

About the Author · · · · · · · · · · · · · · · · · ·

Freddie was born in Dawson, GA. Since his very early years, he has had a passion for God's Word. He has always had a desire to teach the word but like all young people, he had to find himself. In 2015, his path led him overseas and he worked and lived in the Middle East. In 2016, he found the love of his life and it was at that time he made a decision to re-dedicate his life to Christ, not knowing then how he would touch so many different people abroad.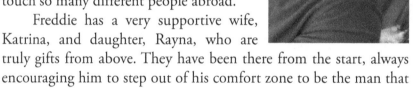

Freddie has a very supportive wife, Katrina, and daughter, Rayna, who are truly gifts from above. They have been there from the start, always encouraging him to step out of his comfort zone to be the man that God as created him to be.

Freddie is very active on social media, always focusing on positive quotes in the hopes that if he could just help one person when they are going through something, he has done something great. His hobbies include having an open dialogue about the Word of God, traveling, watching sports, and spending time with family.

Thank you for all the continued support of his purpose, passion, and journey in life.

All praises to the most high.

CPSIA information can be obtained
at www.ICGtesting.com
Printed in the USA
LVHW090512310721
694023LV00003B/720

9 781636 301327